KINGDOM PROMISES

DEVOTIONS EMPOWERED BY
BIBLICAL STATEMENTS OF FAITH

GOD
WILL

KEN HEMPHILL

PUBLISHING GROUP

NASHVILLE, TENNESSEE

KINGDOM PROMISES:
GOD WILL

Copyright © 2008 by Ken Hemphill
All rights reserved

ISBN 978-0-8054-4768-2

B&H Publishing Group
Nashville, Tennessee
www.BHPublishingGroup.com

Unless otherwise noted, all Scripture quotations
have been taken from the *Holman Christian Standard
Bible*® Copyright © 1999, 2000, 2002, 2003 by
Holman Bible Publishers.

Other Scriptures used include the New American
Standard Bible (NASB) Copyright © 1960, 1962,
1963, 1968, 1971, 1972, 1973, 1975, 1977, 1995 by
The Lockman Foundation. Used by permission.

Dewey Decimal Classification: 242.5
God — Promises / Devotional Literature

Printed in the United States
1 2 3 4 5 12 11 10 09 08

I dedicate this book to:

{
Russ and Cindy Bush
Betty Jo and Larry Lewis
}

Dear friends who have lived out
before the world the truth that
"God Will Dwell Among Us"

In Memory of

L. Russ Bush (1944-2008)
and
Betty Jo Lewis (1943-2008)

Who Now Dwell *with the* King

PREFACE

Studying God's Word always brings its own rewards. I have been deeply moved by the study of these simple statements that are scattered throughout the Word of God. It is my prayer that they will minister in your life as they have mine. I thank you for your willingness to buy this book and allow me to be your guide as the Holy Spirit informs your mind and transforms your heart.

As always, I am indebted to my wife, who is my partner in ministry and my encourager in this ministry of writing. She brings the order and solitude to our home that makes it possible for me to reflect and write. She is often the source of ideas that soon appear in my books. Our devotional times together frequently become theological discussions which enrich my understanding.

My children are a constant joy to me, and our growing family provides a rich context for writing. Tina and Brett have been blessed with a daughter, Lois, who is as active as her "papa." Rachael and Trey have a daughter, Emerson, and a new son, Ward, whose smiles light up a room. Katie and Daniel and their daughter Aubrey are even further blessings from the Lord. My family is the context for my entire ministry.

I want to thank Morris Chapman, the visionary, former leader of the Southern Baptist Convention for calling our denomination to focus on God's kingdom. He gave me freedom to write the things God laid on my heart. All of my colleagues at the Executive Committee of the Southern Baptist Convention have encouraged me in this phase of ministry.

As usual, the good folks at Broadman and Holman have been my partners in this ministry. I am challenged by the trust they place in me and inspired by their integrity. I can't begin to express my gratitude to Lawrence Kimbrough, my partner in this writing adventure. Lawrence is far more than an editor. He is a friend, colleague, and artist. What he does with a rough draft is a thing of beauty.

This book is somewhat of a new genre. It looks like a daily devotional in its format, but it is written to be "bite-sized" theology.

I have attempted to explain each of these great Kingdom Promises in its original context and then to apply it to life. Thus, I highly recommend that you read this book with your Bible open, because the focal passages will have the greatest impact on you as you see them in context. You might also want to consider using these verses as a Scripture memory project while you're reading.

I pray God will use his Word to bring encouragement to your heart. And if this book of Kingdom Promises speaks life to you and ministers to your needs, I hope you'll pass it along to someone else.

Ken Hemphill
Travelers Rest, South Carolina
Spring 2008

GOD WILL
GUIDE YOUR DECISIONS

> **Genesis 24:7** The Lord, the God
> of heaven . . . He will send His
> angel before you.

Have you ever faced a task that seemed impossible? Have you ever sensed God calling you to do something that went beyond your own strength? If so, you might identify with Eliezer, Abraham's servant, who was tasked with finding a wife for Abraham's son, Isaac.

It was the custom in pastoral tribes for the parents to choose a bride for the son, but Abraham's motive was a far higher one. He did not want his son to marry a Canaanite woman. After all, Isaac was the heir of promise; he could not marry a woman who didn't know the true God. The bride must come from within the family of God.

Abraham assigned this task to his loyal servant Eliezer. But Eliezer seemed over-whelmed by the task, and asked, "Suppose the woman is unwilling to follow me to this land? Should I have your son go back to the land you came from?" (Gen. 24:5). How could Eliezer be sure that the parents of the girl would permit her to leave with a stranger and return to a distant land to marry a man they had never met?

Good question!

Abraham insisted that Isaac not leave home, since God had taken Abraham from his father's house and promised him this land. But Abraham was undeterred by the question, for he was certain that "the Lord, the God of heaven," who had provided for him throughout his pilgrimage, would "send His angel" before the servant.

If you read the rest of the story, you discover that Eliezer took gifts for the new bride and prayed for success (verse 12). The assurance of God's providing an angel was no excuse for a lack of preparation and prayer. But God answered the servant's prayer by directing him toward Rebekah, helping him choose her as Isaac's wife, ensuring the purity of Abraham's lineage.

What task has God set before you today? He has promised to send his angel of provision before you! Are you prepared, and have you prayed?

GOD WILL
LET US START AGAIN

{ **Deuteronomy 30:4–5** He will gather you and bring you back from there. . . . He will cause you to prosper. }

As we read the Old Testament stories, we become uncomfortably aware that we as New Testament believers often repeat the same mistakes as did Israel of old.

"Deuteronomy" means the second giving of the law. This was made necessary by the rebellion of the generation that failed to take possession of the Promised Land because of stubborn unbelief. Thus, Deuteronomy does not give a new law, but restates the law for the new generation that would inhabit the land of promise.

In Deuteronomy 29, Moses challenged the people to renew the covenant, then he issued a warning designed to keep them from abandoning the covenant they had made with God. He reminded them of all God had done in the past to deliver them. Then he passionately urged Israel to obey God, setting before them the option of blessing and cursing (verse 1).

Tragically, the history of Israel seems to have a familiar and repeated theme — disobedience leading to their defeat and dispersion among the nations. Yet God held out the opportunity of repentance. "Return to the Lord your God and obey Him with all your heart and all your soul by doing everything I am giving you today" (verse 2). It wasn't simply a matter of sorrowful, well-intentioned words. Repentance was to lead to renewed obedience.

God promised that even if the exiles were scattered to the ends of the earth, he would gather them, bring them back, and restore their prosperity. This flowed from his great compassion for Israel and his desire that they be his chosen instrument for extending blessing to the nations. Israel held the "deed" to the Promised Land, but the key to possessing it was dependent upon their obedience to God's Word.

In 1 Corinthians 10:6, Paul warns us that the failures of Israel should serve as an example to us. Are you living in the presence of God's abundance? If not, why not claim this great "God Will" promise and return to him today?

GOD WILL
HIDE YOU FROM DANGER

> **Psalm 27:5** He will conceal me in His shelter in the day of adversity; He will hide me under the cover of His tent.

Do you ever feel like everyone is out to get you? I know it sounds a little paranoid, but there are days when it just seems we can't get a break and that everything and everyone is marshaled against us.

In the early verses of Psalm 27, David spoke of evildoers who came against him to devour his flesh. He even spoke of the possibility of an army being deployed against him. That's because when God rejected Saul as king and chose David in his place, Saul sent his army to destroy him — the one man who was the imminent threat to his kingly reign. Thus, David's fear was well grounded. Today you may be facing both adversaries and circumstances that seem overwhelming. How should you respond? Let's take a lesson from David.

Listen to the dramatic beginning to Psalm 27 — "The Lord is my light and my salvation — whom should I fear? The Lord is the stronghold of my life — of whom shall I be afraid?" David made two profound declarations about the Lord, followed by two questions. If the Lord is your light, your salvation, and the stronghold of your life, is there anyone or anything you should fear? The answer is an obvious "no one" and "nothing."

How did David summon such courage in the face of opposition? He sought God's presence with passionate intensity. David knew that God's presence was the antidote for all fear. He spoke of God concealing him and covering him with his tent. These images probably relate to the large traveling tent called the Tabernacle, which was the place of worship and the symbol of God's presence among his people.

This tent appeared too flimsy to offer any protection from one's enemy. But it was not so much the substance of the *place* of worship as it was the substance of the *God* of worship. In Psalm 32:7, David declared: "You are my hiding place; You protect me from trouble; You surround me with joyful shouts of deliverance."

Find your shelter in his presence.

GOD WILL
LEAD US ETERNALLY

> **Psalm 48:14** This God,
> our God forever and ever—
> He will lead us eternally.

My wife claims that I am "directionally challenged." Simply stated, I get lost easily. So it was no accident that I ordered a GPS navigational system on my last car to assist me in finding my way. Would you like a "navigator" who can guide you in life and beyond? Good news—God is such a guide.

Mount Zion, the city of God, became a symbol of God's presence and protection for ancient Israel. The psalmist depicted the beauty and power of the holy mountain when he spoke of it rising splendidly as "the joy of the whole earth" (verse 2). When kings came against it, they "froze with fear" and "fled in terror" (verse 5).

But the protection was not in Zion with its towers, ramparts, and citadels. The provision was in God; the city was only a symbol of his presence. Verse 8 is the key to understanding this great "God Will" promise. "Just as we heard, so we have seen." If we compare what God has spoken, we will find that it conforms to what we have seen. In other words, God's Word is absolutely reliable.

Read this psalm in its entirety, and hear the psalmist celebrating God's faithful love, his glorious name, his justice, his righteous judgments. It is not insignificant that he sees God's name and praise reaching to the ends of the earth. God desires that everyone know of his faithful love.

The psalmist then invites his listeners to take a walk around Zion and count its towers and ramparts, to tour its citadels so they could tell the generations to come of God's providential care.

He then pauses to focus on the eternal nature of God, who alone can be described as "forever and ever." This phrase speaks also of God's unchanging love and total reliability. It is this God who will lead us even unto death. Only one who is eternal can guide us in this life and beyond the grave. Do you hear the echoes of Jesus' affirmation to the disciples that he alone is the way, the truth, and the life? Do you know Jesus as your eternal guide?

GOD WILL
SETTLE AND SUPPORT YOU

{ **Psalm 55:22** Cast your burden on the Lord, and He will support you; He will never allow the righteous to be shaken. }

I suppose that nothing hurts worse than being betrayed by a friend, someone you believe to be a peer and a companion. The agonized cry of David in this psalm bursts forth from just such a betrayal.

David's description of his emotional condition bears eloquent testimony to his pain. He spoke of "restless" turmoil and pain (verse 2) which caused his heart to shudder within him. Verse 5 tells us all we need to know—"Fear and trembling grip me; horror has overwhelmed me!" His reaction to such unbearable pressure and pain is not unexpected. He wished that he had wings like a dove so he could just fly away and stay gone forever.

Southwestern Airlines has a series of popular commercials that show people in embarrassing situations. The announcer then asks, "Want to get away?" But the situation David was facing was more than embarrassing. It appeared to him to be life-threatening.

The depth of his pain is explained in verses 12–14. His foe was not an enemy but a peer, a companion, a good friend, a man with whom he shared close fellowship. They had attended worship together. Listen to the description of this man, and see if you can identify with David's pain. "His buttery words are smooth, but war is in his heart. His words are softer than oil, but they are drawn swords" (verse 21).

The turning point is found in verses 16–19. David called out to God, praying with groaning agony of soul every "morning, noon, and night" (verse 17).

He was buoyed, however, by the confidence that God would redeem him no matter how many enemies were aligned against him. Therefore, he cried out to all those who are in pain—"Cast your burden upon the Lord and He will support you!" Whatever your appointed lot, you can cast it on the Lord. You must do the "casting" to discover that the Lord will not allow you to be shaken. Are you "clinging" to your burdens, or "casting" them on the Lord?

GOD WILL
BE YOUR PLACE OF SAFETY

> **Psalm 91:11** He will give His angels orders concerning you, to protect you in all your ways.

We find ourselves at such great risk today that we are bombarded by ads promising protection. Some of the dangers are old ones, such as communicable diseases. Other threats, however, are much newer. A few years ago, none of us would have thought about identity theft. Who would have believed that we would need to shred our trash? We live in a dangerous world. But read the promise of the psalmist again and let it sink in—you have angels to guard you "in all your ways."

This entire psalm echoes the theme of the protection of the Most High God. Listen to verse 1—"The one who lives under the protection of the Most High dwells in the shadow of the Almighty." In verse 2, the psalmist speaks of God as his refuge and his fortress. He goes on to speak of being delivered from the hunter's net and the destructive plague. While the image of a mighty fortress fortifies us, making us feel strong, the image of being gathered under God's wings brings us comfort. God guards us like a mother hen cares for her little chicks.

A key phrase in this psalm is found in verse 9, where the writer speaks of the Lord as our "refuge." Based on this reality, we can face the storms of life assured that no harm can befall us that lies beyond God's ability to care for us through it. "He will give His angels orders" to protect us in every way.

Up to this point, the psalmist had been declaring all that God will do for those who make God their refuge. Notice, though, that the speaker in verses 14–16 is the Lord himself, declaring what "I will do."

We could make an entire list of "God Will" promises in this one psalm, all related to God's protection—God will deliver, he will answer, he will be with us in trouble, he will rescue us, he will satisfy us with long life and show us his salvation.

Why not make God your refuge right now? Commit your way to him. You are safe in his providing, protective presence.

GOD WILL
JUDGE IN RIGHTEOUSNESS

{
Psalm 96:13 He will judge
the world with righteousness
and the peoples with
His faithfulness.
}

Do you ever feel like the world is
spinning wildly out of control? When you
watch the news or read the paper, do you
find yourself wondering about life issues?
Why is there so much evil? Why do the
wicked seem to get ahead in this life? Will
there ever be real justice? If you have ever
had any of these thoughts, you will find
strength in this "God Will" promise.

This psalm falls in the middle of a
group of psalms that herald God as the
rightful King. Verses 1–6 speak of the
King's glory. Such a glorious King deserves
the highest praise from his people; thus, the
psalmist begins his hymn with the threefold
command that we should "sing" and bless
the name of the Lord. Further, we are to
proclaim good tidings of his salvation and
tell of his glory among the nations. Notice
that worship and mission are inextricably
bound together.

In verses 7–9, the threefold repetition of the word "sing" is matched by the threefold command to "ascribe" or "give." In grateful recognition we are to ascribe to the Lord the "glory and strength" that are due his name and "bring an offering" as we come into his courts.

The psalm then progresses to its rightful climax (verses 10–13) as the writer looks to the glorious return of the King. In light of his coming, the message that "the Lord reigns" must be spread among the nations since the entire world will be judged with righteousness.

What will this advent of the King mean? It will mean that "the world is firmly established; it cannot be shaken" (verse 10). Contrast this with the rise and fall of empires and nations throughout history. The disastrous results of the chaos and unrighteousness created by the Fall will be replaced one day by the joy, righteousness, and faithfulness of the King.

I find it comforting and encouraging to know that the righteous King will judge the world in righteousness. When all is finally restored, creation itself will shout for joy.

GOD WILL
BLESS HIS PEOPLE

> **Psalm 115:13** He will bless those who fear the Lord — small and great alike.

I hope you've had the opportunity to see "Amazing Grace," the movie about William Wilberforce's work to abolish slavery in England. If so, you were most certainly moved by his tenacity. William marked the passing of the bill to abolish slavery by meditating on the first verse of this psalm. Listen to its note of victory and praise — "Not to us, Lord, not to us, but to your name give glory because of Your faithful love, because of Your truth." God has more in mind than our happiness when he pours out his blessing on us.

When we hear the word "blessing," we sometimes focus on ourselves. We forget the character of the God who desires to bless. The psalmist, however, began by focusing on the greatness of sovereign God who is in the heavens. He focuses on the omnipotence of God and his concern that the nations know that he alone is true God.

Their gods are the works of men's hands; they cannot speak, hear, smell, feel, walk, or utter a sound. And those who worship them will become "just like them"—dead and useless (verse 8). Thus, the psalmist gives a three-fold injunction that Israel "trust in the Lord" (verses 9–11). Unlike the lifeless idols, the Lord is mindful of his people and desires to bless them.

The words "bless" and "blessed" occur five times in this short section. The blessing of God represents the gift of his presence, his protection, and his provision. Why does God desire to bestow blessing? First, he is a gracious and compassionate Father. But second, he desires to enable his people to be a blessing to the nations.

We cannot ignore that this psalm begins with a passion for the glory of the Lord and a concern for the nations that will become like the false gods they worship. God desires to provide for his people so that the nations will know of his goodness. His blessing is never to be consumed but always conveyed. Thus, when you read the title of this promise, don't think only of yourself. Think also of the nations.

GOD WILL
PROTECT YOUR LIFE

> **Psalm 121:7** The Lord will
> protect you from all harm;
> He will protect your life.

We recently moved to upstate South
Carolina, in large part because of my wife's
cancer diagnosis, and we have experienced
God's provision and tender healing in this
place. The Blue Ridge Mountains rise up
from our backyard. My wife loves to look
up toward the mountains and quote the
beginning of this psalm: "I will lift up mine
eyes unto the hills, from whence cometh
my help. My help cometh from the Lord,
which made heaven and earth (verses 1–2
KJV). The majestic mountains are a constant reminder of his sovereign care.

The psalmist continued his focus on the
constant care of the Lord with his reminder
that God does not slumber nor sleep. He is
our keeper, and as such he will protect us
"from all harm." This does not mean a life
free of challenges and difficulties, but one
of assured conviction. The psalmist, for
example, spoke about walking through

dark valleys, even the valley of the shadow of death, but we can do so with the assurance that God is with us.

No one provides a better commentary on this promise of protection than does the Apostle Paul in Romans 8. After promising that God is at work in everything for those who love him, Paul asked several pointed questions that give us a proper perspective of God's protection: "Who is against us?" "Who can bring an accusation against God's elect?" "Who is the one who condemns?" "Who can separate us from the love of Christ?"

He follows this final question with issues such as tribulation, distress, persecution, famine, nakedness, peril, and sword. His conclusion — "In all these things we are more than victorious through Him who loved us" (Rom. 8:37)

The bottom line for the psalmist, as well as for Paul, was the presence and the love of God. And nothing can separate us from that love.

So relax: "The Lord will protect your coming and going both now and forever" (verse 8). You have his word on that.

GOD WILL
BEAUTIFY THE HUMBLE

> **Psalm 149:4 (NASB)** The Lord
> takes pleasure in His people;
> He will beautify the afflicted
> ones with salvation.

Beauty products have become a growth industry. We long for products to make our hair look shiny and our skin look young. Even a cursory glimpse at the shelves laden with beauty products will tell you that the hunger for beauty knows no bounds in terms of age or gender.

The psalmist, however, tells us of a source of beauty that is more than skin deep. Psalm 149 is the next to last psalm. And because the final psalm has a singular theme repeated in many different forms—"praise the Lord"—this penultimate Psalm becomes all the more important as it prepares us for praise.

Psalm 149 begins with the theme of praise—"Hallelujah! Sing to the Lord a new song." The idea of the "new song" is that it is freshly composed based on the goodness of God, leading us to praise him in song and dance and with instruments.

But the basis of the "new song" in this psalm is found in two interrelated truths—that the Lord "takes pleasure in His people" and will "beautify the afflicted ones with salvation." It is almost too wonderful for words to think that the Lord takes pleasure in his people. The only way I can even begin to relate to this truth is to think of my relationship to my own children. As I watch them grow in maturity, I take deep pleasure in them. Do you daily sense God's pleasure? Earlier, the psalmist noted that, "The Lord values those who fear Him, those who put their hope in His faithful love" (Ps. 147:11). Do you worship the Lord and wait for his loving-kindness?

God's pleasure in his people has led him to "beautify" us with salvation, even in our humble state. The word translated as "salvation" can also mean "victory." One of the men in a church I once served said he could see a visible difference in the countenance of people who were saved, that their face radiated an inner joy and a lack of stress. Could that be one part of the beauty of salvation? Does your heart sense and express that beauty?

GOD WILL
MAKE OUR PATHS STRAIGHT

> **Proverbs 3:6** Think about Him in all your ways, and He will guide you on the right paths.

This promise from the Proverbs is one of the best known texts in all of the Old Testament—one of the most frequently claimed promises. I am afraid that many of us have been guilty of claiming the promise of a "straight path" without considering the significance of "acknowledging God in all our ways."

The very first verse of this chapter alerts us to what is entailed in thinking about and acknowledging God: "My son, don't forget my teaching, but let your heart keep my commands." The commitment of the child of God is not partial but total. Verse 5, which is the immediate context of this promise, defines with clarity what it means to acknowledge God in all our ways. "Trust in the Lord with all your heart, and do not rely on your own understanding." This wholehearted trust only begins when we renounce our "own understanding."

"All your heart" means that the total person with all its inherent choices, decisions, motives, intentions, and ponderings must be submitted to the Father.

But when Solomon said, "Do not rely on your own understanding," he was not endorsing an anti-intellectual approach to life, as if ignorance is bliss. He did mean, however, that we must submit all our knowledge, beliefs, and commitments to God and to His Word. Both our intellectual and practical convictions must be submitted to the wisdom of the Lord. We must forgo attempting to figure out the complexities of life on our own.

In response to our trust in him, the Lord promises to "make straight" or "direct" our steps, to lead us "on the right paths." This suggests both guidance and strength to make progress in the daily affairs of life. We can move through every event of life with the calm assurance that our path is marked out by the Lord, our strength coming from him. Trust me—this is far better than trying to muddle our way through each day based on our own ability to understand the complexities of life.

GOD WILL
REWARD GENEROSITY

> **Proverbs 19:17** Kindness to
> the poor is a loan to the Lord,
> and He will give a reward
> to the lender.

Two themes that echo throughout the
Proverbs are those of hearing instruction
and handling money. Both seem to plague
people of every generation. We are often
inclined to be both stubborn and stingy.
This particular "God Will" promise tells us
that he watches how we use the resources
he provides for us.

When you read through the Proverbs,
you find numerous references to money
and finances, as well as several passages
that deal with the relationship between the
"haves" and the "have nots." In Proverbs
22:7, the writer tells us; "The rich rule over
the poor, and the borrower is a slave to the
lender." In that same context, he speaks of
the "generous person" sharing his food
with the poor (verse 9).

Our gracious response to the poor is
designed to be a reflection of God's great
generosity toward us. But this verse

expresses an even deeper motive for sharing with the poor: when we are gracious to those in need, it is like lending to the Lord.

Does this remind you of the teaching of Jesus concerning the judgment? He indicated that those who are to inherit the kingdom are those who fed him when he was hungry, who gave him drink when he was thirsty, who took him in when he was a stranger, and who cared for and visited him when he was imprisoned. The righteous wonder when they did these things for the Lord. "The King will answer them, 'I assure you: Whatever you did for one of the least of these brothers of Mine, you did for Me'" (Matt. 25:40).

This promise of God—that he will reward the one who gives to the poor—doesn't mean that we will always get our money back dollar for dollar, but it does promise that God will faithfully repay us in a way of his wise choosing. This kingdom promise assures us that the Lord watches and knows all that we do, even the little kindnesses done with no fanfare and with no desire for applause.

GOD WILL
RESCUE FROM INJUSTICE

> **Proverbs 20:22** Don't say,
> "I will avenge this evil!"
> Wait on the Lord, and
> He will rescue you.

"Trust me; I won't forget what you did to me!" "One day, I will get even!" "I will pay you back for that!" Do you ever find yourself saying or even thinking about repaying in kind those who do evil to you? Most of us have done so at some time or another. It is human nature to want to get even. We don't want to think that someone can get by with injustice. But this promise gives us an opportunity to practice our trust in the Lord. Are we willing to allow the Father to make our paths straight?

The first principle of kingdom justice is to commit any perceived grievance to the Lord, who is both all-knowing and entirely just. I suppose the hardest part of this verse is the instruction to "wait on the Lord." We want instant gratification. We want to see evil addressed immediately and to have the personal satisfaction of seeing people get "what they deserve" when they do evil. Of course, we don't want to receive "what we deserve"—we want grace and mercy.

Paul instructs his readers by a similar truth in Romans 12, telling the believers to never take their own revenge but rather to leave room for God's wrath. One of the difficulties with exacting our own revenge is our lack of knowledge and compassion. We often seek revenge only to learn later that we were lacking pertinent details. The Lord lacks no details, however, and thus can repay fairly in every circumstance.

Paul adds further instructions to our understanding of how to deal with evil. We respond to evil with good, to give our enemy food and drink. This response "heaps fiery coals" on our enemies head (Rom. 12:20). This probably means that it may bring our enemy to repentance. Thus by returning good for evil, God enables us to overcome evil with good.

Isn't it good to know that when we receive evil treatment, we can trust God to rescue us? Make this a practice beginning today, and sense your stress level going down in direct proportion.

GOD WILL
ESTABLISH PEACE

{ **Isaiah 2:4** He will settle disputes among the nations and provide arbitration for many peoples. }

Even as a young child, the biblical promise that the nations would "beat their swords into plowshares, and their spears into pruninghooks" grabbed my attention and stimulated my imagination. I didn't fully comprehend the imagery, but I knew that it spoke of a day of peace. The desire for universal peace is the desire of many in every generation, but it seems to become even more elusive as wars and rumors of wars multiply.

Prophets like Isaiah, Micah (4:4), and Joel (3:10) look forward to a day when peace will reign. The phrase "in the last days" in Isaiah 2:2 is a technical expression which looks to the eschatological return and reign of the King. The prophet speaks of a great harvest when "all nations will stream" toward God's presence (verse 2). The peoples from these diverse nations will say, "Come, let us go up to the mountain of the Lord, to the house of the God of Jacob. He will teach us about His ways so that we may walk in His paths" (verse 3).

The issues that have separated nation from nation for generations will not simply disappear. They will only be settled by the supreme judge and King of kings. He will judge between nations, and the decisions he renders will accepted by all. The peace that will reign in that day will be no uneasy truce but will be a lasting peace based on the righteous judgment of the King. "Nations will not take up the sword against other nations, and they will never again train for war" (verse 4). This permanent peace will render all weapons of war obsolete, and the fruitfulness restored in the kingdom will be such that plowshares will be in great demand. These images of a full harvest had great meaning to an agrarian people (see Ezek. 36:23ff).

Does this picture create a longing in your heart? What can we do to bring this picture to its full fruition? We can pray, give, and go to the nations so that every person in every nation has the opportunity to hear that the King of kings gives peace.

GOD WILL
TEND TO HIS FLOCK

{ Isaiah 40:11 (NASB) He will
tend His flock, in His arm
He will gather the lambs and
carry them in His bosom. }

Most trips to the Holy Land include
a mandatory stop at a factory replete with
many unique local gifts to take to friends
who couldn't come along on the trip. One
of the favorites of most tourists is the olive
wood carving of the shepherd carrying his
sheep. It is one of the tenderest images in
all of Scripture.

Isaiah begins the fortieth chapter of
his prophecy with a tender word from God.
"'Comfort, comfort My people,' says your
God" (verse 1). This word of comfort is the
promise of the coming King. We would
expect this King to come with great power,
and we are not disappointed. "See, the
Lord God comes with strength, and His
power establishes His rule" (verse 10).

But while we are awed by his power,
we are also moved by his tenderness, for
he is pictured as a shepherd. The psalmist
pictured the Lord as our "shepherd" who

cares for us (Ps. 23). Isaiah picked up on this comforting picture with three "God Will" promises.

"He will tend His flock." Some translations read "feed His flock," but the word is more inclusive, speaking to his care for all the needs of his sheep.

"He will gather the lambs." When the sheep are weak or injured and cannot move on their own initiative, he will carry them in his arms.

"He will gently lead the nursing ewes." This affirmation points not only to the shepherd's care for the fragile young sheep, but also demonstrates his concern for the continuity of the flock.

We cannot leave this important kingdom promise without recalling that Jesus spoke of himself as the good shepherd. As such, he willingly laid down his life for the sheep. The good shepherd knows his sheep and they know him (John 10:7–15).

Do you know Christ as your good shepherd? Do you listen for his voice speaking tenderly to you? What has he said to you today? Will you obey the words of this one who cares for all your needs?

GOD WILL
BLESS MANY NATIONS

> **Isaiah 52:15** He will sprinkle many nations. Kings will shut their mouths because of Him.

When an Old Testament man sinned and broke the intimate relationship he had with God, the priest would dip his finger in bulls' blood and sprinkle the blood seven times before the veil of the sanctuary. This is a bit foreign to us, but it was crucial to the man under the Old Covenant.

Isaiah picked up this image in looking to the coming of the Messiah King. I would suggest reading the entire chapter, paying special attention to verses 13–15. Isaiah speaks of both the exaltation and humiliation of the coming King. Old Testament man expected his exaltation, but he could hardly comprehend his humiliation.

Isaiah indicated that many would be appalled at the King, that his appearance would be so marred that he would not look like a man. If you saw *The Passion of the Christ* by Mel Gibson, this reality will forever be burned into your memory.

It is nonetheless startling that the prophet declares—"He will sprinkle many nations." We have already noted that the concept of sprinkling was connected with cleansing from sin by the sprinkling of God. The prophet Ezekiel used a similar image to speak of purifying with water. In both contexts, the prophets indicate that the cleansing provided by the blood of the crucified King will be sufficient for all the nations.

In response, kings will shut their mouths, appalled that they had misunderstood so badly the provision God had made for the redemption of all nations. Yet the good news is that through Christ's redemptive sacrifice, they will see and understand what they had not previously been able to comprehend.

The apostle Paul quoted a portion of this verse to defend his missionary activity when he wrote to the Roman believers (Rom. 15:21). God has provided a means for the cleansing of all peoples and nations. And now it is our responsibility to take that good news to the ends of the earth so the nations can see and understand.

GOD WILL
FREELY FORGIVE US

> **Isaiah 55:6–7** Seek the Lord
> while He may be found . . .
> for He will freely forgive.

Are you absolutely certain your sins
have been forgiven? If not, this may be the
kingdom promise you have been waiting to
hear. If so, this promise will remind you of
the goodness of the Lord.

Isaiah begins with the condition for
finding forgiveness. We must "seek the
Lord while He may be found." The word
translated "seek" may be a little too weak.
The idea is that we must cast ourselves
upon the Lord. To seek, then, is not an
issue of idle curiosity or mild interest; it is
the passion of one's life. The person who
understands the gravity of his sin will seek
the Lord with utter abandon. We cannot
be casual about this matter of seeking the
Lord. The brevity of life means that the
opportune time will someday pass.

What, then, does seeking the Lord
entail? It means the "wicked one" must
"abandon" his way and thoughts (verse 7).

In case you are wondering, the term "wicked one" describes all of mankind. Paul would later declare, "For all have sinned and fall short of the glory of God" (Rom. 3:23). The recognition of our sinful condition leads to repentance, which in turn enables us to "return to the Lord" (verse 7). Repentance is not merely the recognition of sin or even sorrow for sin; it is the turning from sin and the turning to God.

Now here's the good news, repeated in slightly different terms: God will "have compassion" on sinful man and "will freely forgive." Can you imagine God being such a merciful God that he will show compassion on sinners like we are and forgive us? We truthfully cannot imagine such grace and mercy. Thus, God reminds us that His thoughts and ways are higher than ours (Isa. 55:8–9), and He promises that his word will accomplish what he desires.

If you have never turned from your sin and turned to him, you can do so right now. He will have compassion on you and freely forgive. If you know this forgiveness, thank him for his mercy.

GOD WILL
REIGN AS KING

{ **Jeremiah 23:5** He will reign wisely as king and administer justice and righteousness in the land. }

We have an ingrained sense of what's fair. We hear it on the playground or in the board room. It's like we have this internal bell that goes off when people treat us unfairly. "That's not fair!" we cry. Wouldn't it be great to have leaders who always did what was right and fair?

The prophet Jeremiah was called upon to deliver messages that were not always pleasant, messages of impending judgment. Nonetheless, God allowed him to declare the good news of a coming King who would act wisely and execute justice and righteousness in the land.

This message of a just, righteous king must have stood out in stark contrast to the foolish kings of Israel who were like shepherds that scattered their flock and had not attended to them (verses 1–2). These introductory verses are like an epilogue of denunciation of the four kings mentioned in Jeremiah 21 and 22. The historical Davidic dynasty was at an end. and the people of God were headed for Babylonian captivity. But there was a future! God declared that he would raise up shepherds over them who would cast away their fear. The days were coming when God would raise up a righteous, legitimate shoot from the branch of David (verse 5). "This is what He will be named: The Lord Is Our Righteousness" (verse 6).

This message was likely delivered during the reign of King Zedekiah, whose name ironically means "the Lord is my righteousness." Tragically, however, the king failed to live up to his name or his potential. But there would be a new King whose name is "The Lord Our Righteousness" (Jehovah Tsidkenu).

This name points to the time when all men will recognize that God alone is the source of righteousness. In 1 Corinthians, Paul declares that Jesus has become our righteousness—our Jehovah Tsidkenu! Do you know the King who reigns with righteousness? Is he *your* righteousness? Does your life demonstrate his reign?

GOD WILL
PLEAD OUR CASE

> **Jeremiah 50:34** Their Redeemer is strong; the Lord of Hosts is His name. He will fervently plead their case.

Courtroom drama has always fascinated us. I can still remember watching Perry Mason when I was a child. I knew that if I was ever faced with going before a jury, I wanted him on my side. Any one of us would want the best lawyer possible to be our advocate.

The Israelites and Judeans were being held captive by a people who refused to release them. "All their captors hold them fast," Jeremiah reported, underlining the helplessness of their plight (verse 33). God had allowed them to be taken into captivity in Babylon because of their disobedience. How could they expect to be released from bondage when they were held captive by a host of Babylonians much stronger as a nation than the captives of Israel?

First, Jeremiah assured them their redeemer was stronger than their enemies. God who allowed their captivity to bring judgment will now be their "redeemer." The term "redeemer" would remind them of a provision that allowed a relative to adopt or "redeem" a family member or possessions (see Ruth 4). The use of this term emphasized the family bond of God and his people. Their redemption would be both personal and costly.

The declaration that "the Lord of hosts is His name" serves as a reminder that God is sovereign over all nations whether they recognize him as such or not. The hosts of Babylonian captors were no match for the Lord of Hosts.

Finally, Jeremiah assured them that "He will fervently plead their case." The image is from the court of justice. Not only was God their advocate, but he had committed to plead their case thoroughly and effectually. God's deliverance would be the result of his own righteousness.

The result of the case is secure. God gives his people rest which, in turn, gives his enemies unrest—a play on words in the Hebrew which can be detected in most English translations. It is comforting to know that God will plead our cause!

GOD WILL
DELIVER US

> **Daniel 3:17 (NASB)** Our God
> whom we serve is able to de-
> liver us . . . and He will deliver
> us out of your hand, O king.

Not many Bible stories are more
popular than the account of Daniel and the
den of lions. I can still recall my childhood
fascination as my Sunday school teacher
retold the story of three teenagers who
dared to defy a pagan king. I wondered,
could I show such courage and character
in the context where God placed me?

During the third year of the reign of
Jehoiakim, the king and the cream of the
population of Israel were taken into
Babylonian captivity by Nebuchadnezzar.
The pagan king selected the best of the
Jewish young people to serve in his court,
including Daniel and three of his friends,
who exhibited great courage when they
refused to eat the king's food (1:8). This
refusal to compromise personal convictions
led to an experiment that revealed these
young men were ten times better than the
magicians in the king's realm (1:20).

Daniel was promoted for his wisdom and his God-given ability to interpret the king's dreams (chap. 2). Yet the inevitable conflict was on the horizon. Nebuchadnezzar made a gold idol of huge proportions and gave orders that everyone fall down and worship it. Failure to worship would be punishable by death in a blazing furnace (3:6). Daniel and his three friends refused to worship the image, and the Chaldeans soon reported them to the king.

The king called Shadrach, Meshach, and Abed-nego before him and gave them one last chance to worship the idol. Their response is the "God Will" promise above. Yet if you read verse 18, you find that their faith contains no presumption. The Jewish teens were unwilling to compromise even if God chose not to deliver them.

Would you like to possess such a powerful faith that you can stand against the tide of conformity and display godly character? The key is found in Daniel 11:32. "The people who know their God will be strong and take action." The more you know about God through his Word, the greater will be your faith.

GOD WILL
REFRESH LIKE THE RAIN

> **Hosea 6:3** He will come to us like the rain, like the spring showers that water the land.

Do you ever feel spiritually parched—just too dry to produce any spiritual fruit? You need the spring showers of the Lord. My dad loved his yard work; he took great joy in seeing his plants grow. He loved the spring rain and the promise it held. I must have inherited this love from him because I find nothing more refreshing than a gentle spring shower.

The prophet Hosea's marriage to an unfaithful wife became a picture of Israel's spiritual unfaithfulness toward their loving God. The people of the Northern Kingdom had left God and joined themselves to Baal. Nonetheless, God desired to redeem them in the same manner that Hosea was willing to buy back his faithless wife.

After the stinging rebuke for their spiritual adultery in chapter 5, Hosea looked toward the day when Israel would return to the Lord. In the first three verses of chapter 6, exhortation is immediately followed by a promise.

In verse 1, the Israelites were exhorted to "return to the Lord," acknowledging that God had torn and wounded them for their rebellion. Yet he would heal, bandage, revive, and raise them up, enabling them to "live in His presence" (verse 2). No doubt you will notice a multiplicity of "God Will" promises in this powerful section.

The second exhortation, in verse 3, is to "strive" or "press on" to know the Lord, which literally means "to pursue or chase." It signifies the intensity and passion of their desire to know the Lord. God's response to such passion is "as certain as the dawn." He will come "like the rain."

You may wonder why the repetition of the promise of rain. It is likely that Hosea was referring to the promise of both winter and spring rain. If you read Deuteronomy 11:13–14, you will find God's promise that he will give the early and the late rain to ensure a bountiful harvest.

Do you desire a fruitful Christian life? If you thirst for the early and the late rain, you must "press on to know the Lord."

GOD WILL
DEAL WITH DISOBEDIENCE

{ **Micah 1:3 (NASB)** The Lord is
coming forth from His place.
He will come down and tread
on the high places of the earth. }

Israel often looked to the day of the
coming of the Lord as a sublime event,
bringing deliverance. But while the return
of the King will be a day of redemption, it
will also be a day of judgment for those
who have ignored his Word. The New
Testament also speaks of the day of the
Lord's return in terms of judgment.

The prophet Micah summoned all the
peoples of the earth to heed his warning
(verse 2). By calling upon all the peoples,
he once again underlined an oft-ignored
truth—God alone is God, and thus all the
peoples of the earth will be accountable to
him. When we fully comprehend this single
truth, it will cause us to have a passion to
take the good news to the ends of the earth.

Phrases such as "coming forth" and
"come down" describe the personal inter-
vention of the Creator/King in man's global
affairs. Do we need to be reminded that he

is the sovereign Lord of history, nations, heaven, and earth? Sometimes we are lulled into thinking that the events of history are nothing more than "the rule of the strongest," but above and beyond all historical events, God is still sovereign.

Micah pictures the returning King as treading on the high places of the earth. This may simply be a picturesque way of describing his greatness. Like a massive giant, he steps from mountain to mountain as they melt under him and the valleys split from his footfall (verse 4). There can be no doubt that the Bible teaches the dissolution of the earth at his return (Heb. 12:26–29). "High places" could also refer to pagan shrines and idolatrous worship. Notice that Micah speaks of Jerusalem as the "high place of Judah" (verse 5). Is he suggesting their worship had degenerated to the point that it was little more than pagan idolatry?

We love to focus on the "God Will" promises which are most comforting, but we can't ignore the truth that he will "tread on the high places." Do we have any high places of rebellion and disobedience in our lives? Ask him to remove them today.

GOD WILL
STAND AND SHEPHERD US

> **Micah 5:4** He will stand and
> shepherd them in the strength
> of Yahweh, in the majestic
> name of Yahweh His God.

I have always loved Christmas pageants. Many churches today have splendid productions of the birth of the Messiah King. When I was a child, our costumes were little more than mom's bathrobe, a shepherd's crook, and a few pair of angel's wings. Yet the story never changes nor does it cease to amaze—the sovereign King coming to earth in such humble circumstances. This "God Will" promise occurs in a context that takes us back to those simple Christmas stories.

Micah declared that Israel's deliverance from their long travail would coincide with the appearance of the Messiah as redeemer, coming from Bethlehem Ephrathah. "You are small among the clans of Judah," he said of the city. Yet out of Bethlehem would come One to be ruler in Jerusalem. He is no ordinary deliverer: "His origin is from antiquity, from eternity" (verse 2).

In verse 3, Micah spoke of one who was in labor, bearing a child. The first hearers may have heard this prophecy in terms of Israel's restoration being likened to the delay and the pangs of childbirth. But there can be little doubt that this prophecy had in mind the virgin mother mentioned by his contemporary, Isaiah (7:14). In the very next verse, the prophet spoke of this child in very personal terms.

He will "shepherd" God's people, something the earthly leaders of Israel had failed to do. Further, he would do so in the "strength" of the Lord and the majesty of his name. No one other than Jesus could fit this wonderful description.

But this promised redeemer would not simply restore *Israel*, for "His greatness will extend to the ends of the earth." Israel continually neglected the truth that God's heartbeat has always been that all the nations of the earth come to know him as their rightful King. Israel failed to understand that their calling was to be on mission with him to the ends of the earth. Does our praying, giving, and going indicate that *we* are on mission with him?

GOD WILL
BRING US INTO THE LIGHT

> **Micah 7:9** He will bring
> me into the light; I will
> see His salvation.

Many people have a fear of the dark.
Much that is evil takes place under the
cloak of darkness. Jesus declared: "This,
then, is the judgment: the light has come
into the world, and people loved darkness
rather than the light because their deeds
were evil" (John 3:19).

Babylonian captivity and the fall of
Jerusalem sunk Israel into the depths of
darkness. Yet in his nation's darkest hour,
the prophet Micah expressed his confidence in the faithfulness of God and in his
ability to redeem Israel. In verse 7, Micah
declared his intention to watch and wait
for the Lord with the assurance that God
would hear him.

He then warned his enemies not to
gloat about their apparent victory. You
might wonder how he could sound such
a positive note in such a dark hour. It's
because his captors had not yet heard the

end of the story: "Though I have fallen, I will stand up; though I sit in darkness, the Lord will be my light" (verse 8). To confess that the Lord is light is to declare that he is the source of all goodness. The psalmist put it this way: "The Lord is my light and my salvation—whom should I fear? The Lord is the stronghold of my life—of whom should I be afraid?" (Ps. 27:1).

The turning point from darkness and despair to light and hope is the recognition of sin and the desire for deliverance. As Micah declared: "Because I have sinned against Him, I must endure the Lord's rage" (verse 9). Israel's captivity was the consequence of their own sin and rebellion. The prophet acknowledged this on behalf of the people. But notice there is a glorious "until" in this verse: "until He argues my case and establishes justice for me." God will bring his people "into the light" and demonstrate his righteousness. In spite of their rebellion, God has been faithful to his covenant promise.

If you desire to come out of darkness into light, agree with him about your sin problem. Allow him to plead your case.

GOD WILL
CAST OUR SINS AWAY

> **Micah 7:19** You will cast all our sins into the depths of the sea.

One distinctive of the Christian religion is that it provides the solution for man's sin problem. When you study other world religions, you find that they have no answer for this universal problem; thus, man can never be confident of his forgiveness and salvation. Yet I find that many Christians struggle with guilt over forgiven sin. Here is a promise for you!

In the context of this verse, Micah ponders—"Who is a God like You, removing iniquity and passing over rebellion?" (verse 18). The obvious point is that there is none like our God! The reason that he does not retain his anger over sin forever is that he "delights" in loving us (verse 18). What an incredible truth to ponder! It was God's faithful, unchanging love that sent Jesus to earth to undo the power of sin, enabling us not to perish but to live with God forever (John 3:16).

Micah suggests that God's tenderness is like that of a nurturing mother. But the images of what our compassionate God does to sin demonstrates his awesome power. To "vanquish" or to "tread under foot" is to defeat our sin with absolute finality. Sin is pictured as an enemy, with God as the conqueror who has defeated sin and liberated his people from its power and its consequences. Our sin will not cast us into the despair of guilt, for he has taken away its power, and it can no longer have dominion over us!

As if this isn't enough, Micah adds that God will cast all our sins into the depths of the sea. The imagery may be that of hurling Pharaoh's chariots into the Red Sea where they sank like the proverbial rock. Hurling into the sea speaks of both complete, total forgiveness and the removal of all guilt forever.

Here's what God does with our sin. He puts it out of sight (Isa. 38:17), out of reach (Ps. 103:12), out of mind (Jer. 31:34), and out of existence (Isa. 43:25; Acts 3:19). No one has the right to resurrect what God has buried in the sea!

GOD WILL
CHASE AWAY HIS ENEMIES

{ **Nahum 1:8** He will chase
His enemies into darkness. }

Do you ever watch the evening news
and think, "How does a loving and just
God allow such great evil?" You are not
alone. Israel often wondered the same
thing, so God sent his prophets to put
world events into biblical focus.

The prophet Nahum lived during the
fall and destruction of the Assyrian empire,
which was assured by the fall of Nineveh
in 612 BC. Nahum's name means "consolation," and Israel certainly needed a word of
consolation. Assyria was one of the most
cruel and ruthless nations of the ancient
world. They destroyed and burned cities,
then subjected the conquered inhabitants
to all manner of indignities.

The prophecy of Nahum assures us
that God is not remote and unconcerned
when it comes to world events. Nahum
begins by a threefold reminder that God is
an "avenging God" (verse 2). Yet his anger

is not like ours. It is righteous and just. So while he is great in power, he is slow to anger. We are often guilty of mistaking God's patience for a lack of justice. We cry out that God is not fair when we see the guilty going unpunished. Yet the prophet assures the reader—"The Lord will never leave the guilty unpunished" (verse 3).

The prophet goes on to demonstrate God's power over all the earth and its peoples with a simple conclusion: "Who can withstand His indignation? Who can endure His burning anger?" (verse 6). Yet our awesome God is also completely just. He is "good, a stronghold in the day of distress" (verse 7). He knows those who take refuge in him. But a just God cannot leave the guilty unpunished. Thus, Nahum repeats the word of judgment, declaring that God will "completely destroy" Nineveh (verse 8). The capital of godless Assyria would be no more.

We are sometimes guilty of over-sentimentalizing God, suggesting he will not bring judgment or cast sinners into hell. God is just and cannot overlook sin. Yet he is a refuge for those who know him.

GOD WILL
SPEAK TO YOU

{ **Habakkuk 2:1** I will watch to
see what He will say to me. }

A favorite verse from the book of
Habakkuk is 1:5—"Look at the nations
and observe—be utterly astounded! For
something is taking place in your days that
you will not believe when you hear about
it." We usually quote this verse positively
concerning God's desire to do something
wonderfully new. That is certainly true and
appropriate when it comes to God. Yet the
new "something" in the original context is
God's plan to use the Chaldeans to punish
his own disobedient people.

In the remainder of chapter 1, the
prophet struggled with the apparent
success of the Chaldeans. He wondered
whether they would "continually slaughter
nations without mercy" (verse 17).

How do you respond to events of life
when you can't fully comprehend them?
Habakkuk took a proactive approach. He
declared his intention of taking up his

position on the rampart. Like a sentry, he would be vigilant on his watch. What was he looking to see? "I will watch to see what He will say to me," certain that God would speak to him. Even though he knew the Lord's words might contain reproof, he desired to hear from God. And he didn't have to wait long.

God declared to Habakkuk that his judgment was certain, using a series of statements that begin with the word "woe." The bottom line—"But the Lord is in His holy temple; let everyone on earth be silent in His presence" (2:20). You can trust the Lord to be faithful to his Word!

But while we are waiting, the righteous are called to live by faith (verse 4). God is totally trustworthy, and therefore you can trust him to run the world. It's not your job! Habakkuk said that even if everything seems to be shaken, "Yet I will triumph in the Lord; I will rejoice in the God of my salvation!" (3:18). That is what it means to live by faith.

When you don't understand the events of life, you can be confident that the Lord will speak to you.

GOD WILL
QUIET YOU IN HIS LOVE

> **Zephaniah 3:17** He will
> rejoice over you with gladness.
> He will bring you quietness
> with His love.

Between the godly kings Hezekiah
and Josiah, the people of God experienced
a period of religious and moral decline.
And either before or during the reign of
Josiah, the young king who rediscovered
the scrolls of God's Word and instituted
much needed change among the nation,
Zephaniah delivered the above message.
It is a message of judgment tempered by
a reminder of God's covenant love.

The unifying theme of the book is the
day of the Lord, which Zephaniah depicted
as a day of judgment. Listen to his description of that day: "That day is a day of
wrath, a day of trouble and distress, a day
of destruction and desolation, a day of
darkness and gloom, a day of clouds and
blackness" (1:15).

He pled with his hearers to turn back
to God before the day of his anger neared.
"Seek the Lord, all you humble of the

earth, who carry out what He commands. Seek righteousness, seek humility; perhaps you will be concealed on the day of the Lord's anger" (2:3).

But the prophet found hope in God's promise of a remnant. "I will leave a meek and humble people among you" (3:12) who will trust in the Lord, "will no longer do wrong or tell lies" (verse 13). The remnant is always marked by righteousness.

So in an unexpected celebration, the prophet called upon the daughter of Zion to rejoice and exult with all their heart. What could elicit such joy? The promise that the Lord will be in their midst is twice repeated. God is pictured as a victorious warrior who brings salvation.

But while we expect the image of a warrior, perhaps we are unprepared by the tenderness of this victorious warrior. The seventeenth verse echoes three "God Will" promises that express both joy and compassion. In the midst of celebration arises the promise of a quiet love.

Do you need to sense that quiet love today? Then follow Zephaniah's direction and seek the Lord with all your heart.

GOD WILL
SIT ON HIS THRONE

> **Zechariah 6:13** He will build the Lord's temple; He will be clothed in splendor and will sit on His throne and rule.

Images of the coming King are common in the Old Testament. The prophet Zechariah certainly had his share, speaking often of "that day" or "the day of the Lord." Some of these refer to the first coming of the King (the Incarnation) while others await the second and victorious coming of the rightful King of all the nations.

In this section, Zechariah records a visionary experience of four chariots which represent the four spirits of heaven "going out after presenting themselves to the Lord of the whole earth" (6:5). This is followed by a prophecy of an unusual coronation. The prophet was to go to the house of Josiah, where exiles had gathered, take up an offering, then make an ornate crown from the gold and silver to set on the head of Joshua, the high priest (verses 9–11).

Joshua, the first recipient of the crown, was to take the crown and offer it to a man whose name is Branch, who would "build the Lord's temple" (verse 12). All of the "God Will" promises of verse 13 point to the restoration of this temple and the leadership in Judah, suggesting a renewal of the kingdom of God in the world. But there is clearly more involved in this prophecy than just rebuilding an earthly temple and a rejuvenated government.

The dual coronation of civil and priestly leader is clearly symbolic since it would have been illegal in the Persian colony of Judah. The final fulfillment awaits the day when one man will fulfill both roles of priest and King. "There will also be a priest on His throne, and there will be peaceful counsel between the two of them" (verse 13). Notice further that when this prophecy is fulfilled, all the world's nations will be brought under divine rule. "People who are far off will come and build the Lord's temple" (verse 15).

Isn't it great to know that the rightful King and the great High Priest—Jesus the Christ—is coming to sit on his throne and to rule over all the nations? This should give you hope in a turbulent world.

GOD WILL
PROCLAIM PEACE

> **Zechariah 9:10** He will
> proclaim peace to the nations.
> His dominion will extend
> from sea to sea.

One of the most beloved images in all of Scripture is of Christ entering Jerusalem on the back of a humble donkey. The crowd no doubt picked up on the prophetic imagery, casting palm branches before him as cries of "hosanna" echoed down through the valley.

This prophetic word comes from Zechariah 9:10. The daughter of Zion was told to rejoice greatly and shout in triumph. The cause for celebration — "See, your King is coming to you; He is righteous and victorious, humble and riding on a donkey, on a colt, the foal of a donkey" (verse 9). Yes, the warlike atmosphere of verses 1–8 gives way to the thrilling sounds of celebration in verses 9–10.

The victor is "just and endowed with salvation" (verse 9, NASB). "Just" describes both his character and his reign, a reign that will bring salvation to mankind. But these military images are somewhat interrupted by the image of the King riding on a donkey, suggesting a peaceful entrance. Some commentators think the imagery suggested by a donkey (rather than a mighty stallion) is to further underline the theme of humility. This non-military and non-political imagery would have been a shock to the system of those who had interpreted kingdom promises in terms of political independence for Israel.

This peaceful entrance is further emphasized in verse 10, the locus for our "God Will" promise. The prophet speaks of cutting off chariots and horses of war as the King speaks peace to the nations. As surprising as the theme of peace would have been to some, the universal implications must have been absolutely stunning. The King's dominion will be from sea to sea and to the ends of the earth.

If you know Christ as your personal King, you are part of a worldwide kingdom movement. Does this give you a sense of awe? Have you ever told anyone about your King who will bring peace to the nations?

GOD WILL
PURIFY AND REFINE US

> **Malachi 3:3** He will purify the
> sons of Levi and refine them
> like gold and silver.

When you were a child, did you ever question the wisdom or authority of your parents? We all did, but as we grew more mature, we recognized our attitude to be the height of folly. Malachi wrote during a time of great spiritual lethargy which had impacted every arena of life. Divorce was rampant and social ills were commonplace. Nonetheless, arrogant Israel hurled question after question toward the throne room of heaven.

In the second verse of the book, God declared his covenant love for his people, and yet they responded, "How have You loved us?" The tone was set. The kingdom promise for today is found in the context of another question: "Where is the God of justice?" (2:17). Israel suggested that God was unjust for failing to bring judgment upon their enemies. Have you ever felt that way? Keep reading.

God declared that the day of the Lord is certain. Many of the prophets spoke of it as being judgment poured out on the nations, thus bringing deliverance to Israel. Malachi, however, focused on Israel and the Levites, its leaders and teachers. In light of God's justice, the questions — "Who can endure the day of His coming? And who can stand when He appears? — are stark reminders of our own sinfulness.

The image of the refiner's fire combined with the fuller's soap emphasizes the thoroughness and severity of his cleansing. The refiner sits before the crucible, keeping his eye on the metal to ensure that only the dross is removed. He knows the metal is pure when he can see his own image in the molten metal. When the sons of Levi are fully refined, they will "present offerings to the Lord in righteousness" (verse 3).

God brings judgment upon his own people to refine them in his own image, so that they may serve him in righteousness. This is also a sober reminder that God's judgment will bring ultimate destruction on the unrighteous while it purifies his own children for kingdom service.

GOD WILL
RESTORE OUR HEARTS

{ **Malachi 4:6** He will turn the hearts of fathers to their children and the hearts of children to their fathers. }

In our last promise, we read of the day of the Lord. Malachi picked up that theme once more before completing his prophecy, declaring it "the great and awesome day of the Lord" (verse 5). It is not insignificant that this was God's final word for nearly 400 years, or that one of the first to break the silence was an Elijah-like prophet who cried out, "Repent, because the kingdom of heaven has come near" (Matt. 3:2).

He looked first at the impact of the judgment on the "arrogant and everyone who commits wickedness" (verse 1). They will be like chaff set ablaze, "not leaving them root or branches." The contrast between the evildoer and those who fear God's name could not be more marked. "But for you who fear My name, the sun of righteousness will rise with healing in its wings, and you will go out and playfully jump like calves from the stall" (verse 2).

In Luke 1:17, the angelic messenger quoted this prophecy as he prepared Zacharias for the birth and ministry of John the Baptist. Yet when Elijah appeared with Christ on the Mount of Transfiguration, the disciples asked about the coming of Elijah. On that occasion, Jesus spoke of Elijah's coming in the future to restore all things (Matt. 17:11). Nonetheless, he affirmed that John the Baptist had also fulfilled the ministry of Elijah, yet men had not responded to his ministry. Therefore, there would be another forerunner yet to come.

We are once again given a glimpse at the long-suffering patience of God, "not wishing any to perish" (2 Pet. 3:9). God continues to give an opportunity for us to turn to him in repentance, which will impact our homes and restore broken relationships. But we can't ignore the final words of Malachi's prophecy. If one does not respond with humble contrition, the day of the Lord will "strike the land with a curse" (verse 6). Are you prepared for the coming of the Lord? Have you turned from your sin and accepted God's forgiveness?

GOD WILL
SAVE US FROM OUR SINS

> **Matthew 1:21** You are to name
> Him Jesus, because He will
> save His people from their sins.

What's in a name? Expectant parents
often agonize for months to find a name
that will express their hopes and desires
for their child. This was especially true for
Jewish parents. The child in this story is
actually named by God, which gives his
name even greater significance.

Mary and Joseph were engaged to
be married, and Mary was found to be
pregnant. Joseph, being a righteous and
gracious man, determined to send her
away secretly (verse 19). But God changed
Joseph's mind and his plans by sending an
angelic messenger to explain that Mary had
not been unfaithful. The child that she was
bearing had been supernaturally conceived
by the instrumentation of the Holy Spirit.
Thus, Joseph was to take Mary as his wife.

The angel also told Joseph what they
were to name the child—"Jesus." His name
in the Hebrew, *Yeshua*, means "Yahweh is

salvation." His ministry was to deliver people from their sins. While many in Israel were looking for political redemption, what Israel needed most was personal redemption. Sin and rebellion had led to alienation from holy God, and the birth of this child would provide the answer to every man's problem.

The angel assured Joseph that the birth of Jesus was in keeping with God's eternal plan for redemption. Nearly 700 years earlier, the prophet Isaiah had declared that a virgin would bear a son who would be called "Immanuel," which means "God with us." God's solution for man's greatest problem was to become one with us. He took upon himself human flesh to save us from our sins. Only one who had both the nature of man and the nature of God could provide the redemption of sinful man. Jesus lived a sinless life but died a sinner's death to deliver us from sin.

Have you accepted God's solution for your sin problem? Do you know Jesus as your personal Savior? If you are not sure, you might want to turn to the final pages of this book.

GOD WILL
BAPTIZE WITH THE SPIRIT

> **Matthew 3:11** He Himself
> will baptize you with the
> Holy Spirit and fire.

John the Baptist preached a dramatic message that drew large crowds: "Repent, because the kingdom of heaven has come near" (verse 2). Crowds were not only drawn to him; they responded to his bold message by confessing their sins and being baptized (verse 6). Nonetheless, he refused to baptize those who had not produced fruit in keeping with repentance.

Even though John was growing in popularity, he made it clear that his ministry was only paving the way for one who was so much greater than himself, he did not consider himself worthy of removing the other man's sandals (one of the most menial tasks of a slave). John was preparing a remnant for the coming Messiah.

While John had baptized them in water in response to their repentance for their sins, Jesus would baptize them with the Holy Spirit and fire. Those hearing these words would have remembered the prophesies of Joel (2:28–29) and Malachi (3:2–5). Joel had spoken of the outpouring of the Holy Spirit in the coming kingdom. Malachi had spoken of a judgment of fire.

Both John and Jesus preached repentance and the coming of the kingdom, and both baptized with water as an outward sign of an inward change (see John 4:1–2), but only Jesus offered baptism with the Holy Spirit. Baptism with the Holy Spirit is mentioned on six other occasions in the New Testament, five of which refer to John's declaration. The other is found in 1 Corinthians 12:13. The baptism of the Holy Spirit is an event common to all those who turn from their sin and believe in Christ. The Holy Spirit convicts of sin, grants newness of life, and incorporates the new believer into the body of Christ.

The reference to fire speaks of the purifying and cleansing work of the Holy Spirit in the life of the believer, as well as the sure judgment for those who reject the Holy Spirit's witness to Christ. They will be like chaff that is burned up with unquenchable fire.

GOD WILL
SEND FORTH HIS ANGELS

> **Matthew 24:31** He will send out
> His angels with a loud trumpet,
> and they will gather His elect
> from the four winds.

The topic of the second coming has
created much speculation in the church.
It is unlikely we will settle questions of
dispute in these few paragraphs, but we
can find great encouragement from this
wonderful kingdom promise.

The Lord's coming is pictured as being
sudden, unexpected, visible, and spectacu-
lar. His return will be accompanied by
unusual display in the heavenlies as the sun
and moon are darkened and the stars fall
from the sky. It is possible that this heavenly display actually points to the over-
throw of the cosmic and demonic powers,
often associated with sun, moon, and stars.

Matthew mentions that all the nations
(tribes) will "mourn" (verse 30). This
"mourning" alludes to Zechariah 12:10,
but is here related to the realization that
the day of opportunity has passed and
judgment is imminent.

The appearance on the clouds "with power and great glory" (verse 30) offers a clear contrast to his voluntary humiliation on the cross. The victory and tenderness of the reigning King will be displayed in the sending of his angels for the gathering of the elect from all points of the compass and from one end of the sky to the other. The triumphant Lord will return with all the believers who are already present with him in heaven and will gather his faithful believers here on earth.

The "elect" are those who have pre-pared for his return by responding to the message of redemption prior to his return. Those prepared for his return will be marked by faithful service to the King— "That slave whose master finds him work-ing when he comes will be rewarded" (verse 46). The later half of chapter 24 is a clarion call to the readers of every genera-tion to be ready for his coming. It will be like the time of Noah, when everyone went about the routine affairs of life until the very day that Noah entered the ark.

Are you ready? Will you celebrate his coming and be gathered by his angels?

GOD WILL
REIGN FROM HIS THRONE

> **Matthew 25:31** When
> the Son of Man comes in His
> glory . . . then He will sit on
> the throne of His glory.

There are few pictures more regal or
defining than a king sitting on his throne.
Matthew allows us a brief glimpse into the
throne room of the victorious King of
kings. The picture is certainly one of
grandeur, majesty, authority, and judgment.

All the nations will be gathered before
him since he is the rightful King of all the
peoples of the earth. The King will not only
judge all people groups, but he will judge
persons individually. The phrase "He will
separate them one from another" (verse 32)
indicates that judgment is based on each
individual's earthly response to the King.

Separating the sheep from the goats
clearly recalls Ezekiel 34:17–19. Palestin-
ian shepherds frequently allowed the sheep
and goats to graze together in the same
fields. They could be similar in appearance,
particularly from a distance. Putting the
sheep at his right was the place of honor.

The King then personally addresses those on his right, "Come, you who are blessed by My Father, inherit the kingdom prepared for you from the foundation of the world" (verse 34). Yes, the coming kingdom was prepared for his sheep from before the beginning of creation.

Once again, the sheep demonstrate the validity of their relationship with the King by their service to him and his people while on earth (verses 35–40). This text does not teach "salvation by works," but it clearly teaches that authentic relationship with the King will be demonstrated in one's service to the King while on earth. Paul taught this same truth in Ephesians 2:10, where he indicated that we were "created" for good works. This follows immediately on his declaration that we are saved by grace through faith. Even faith is not an effort of our own but a gift of God.

If you have responded to God's good news in Christ by faith, you will be prepared for the coming King and his eternal kingdom. The tragedy is that many people who claim to be Christians live this life as if this earth is all there is.

GOD WILL
SUFFER MANY THINGS

> **Mark 9:12** Is it written about
> the Son of Man that He must
> suffer many things and be
> treated with contempt?

When I was a minister to youth, I
would take our young people to camp just
before they were prepared to return to
school. We would often have a profound
visitation from the Lord. The teens were
often frightened by the prospect of leaving
the "spiritual security" of the camp and
going back to the real world.

Jesus took Peter, James, and John to
a high mountain where he was transfigured
before them, "His clothes became daz-
zling—extremely white" (verse 3). The
drama was not yet complete, however.
"Elijah appeared to them with Moses, and
they were talking with Jesus" (verse 4).
The disciples, not knowing what to say,
offered to build three tabernacles for Jesus
and his two guests. The Father then drew
their focus to the central character as he
speaks from the heavenlies, "This is My
beloved Son; listen to Him!" (verse 7).

No sooner had they heard the voice than they found themselves alone with Jesus.

On their way down the mountain, Jesus gave them orders not to tell anyone what they had seen until the Son of Man was raised from the dead. One wonders if the disciples were still in a state of shock from these events. They seized upon Jesus' statement to discuss what "rising from the dead" meant and why the scribes indicated that Elijah must come first?

Jesus said that Elijah *would* come first and restore all things. Yet it is clear that the suffering of the Elijah figure is not the central issue. Surely, they were reluctant to believe that the Messiah, whom they had just seen in his transfigured glory, would have to suffer and die. You may recall that Peter was brazen enough to rebuke Jesus for indicating that he must suffer and die (Mark 8:31–33).

The vision of Christ's ultimate glory must wait until his resurrection. Before they could focus on his glory, they must first endure his suffering. He suffered the indignities of our sin that we might one day behold his glory.

GOD WILL
BE CALLED GREAT

> **Luke 1:32** He will be great and
> will be called the Son of the
> Most High.

The angelic messenger not only quieted
Mary's fear when he announced her as the
mother of Jesus; he also declared to her
five great truths about her soon-to-be-born
child. We will discover several wonderful
"God Will" kingdom promises in these
powerful verses.

He will be great. Zacharias was told that
his son John would be great (verse 15),
but the greatness of Mary's son would be
unparalleled by the rest of humanity. His
greatness reflects the greatness which
belongs only to God.

He will be called the Son of the Most High.
John is described as the "prophet of the
Most High" (Luke 1:76), whereas Jesus is
declared as the "Son of the Most High."
The fact that Jesus will be called "Son of
the Most High" points to his equality with
God. "Son of" is often used to refer to one
who possesses his father's qualities. Jesus

as the Son of the Most High possesses all the qualities of God the Father.

The Lord will give him the throne of his father David. Jesus, as David's descendant, will sit on David's throne when he begins His millennial reign. This promise focuses on Jesus' role as Israel's rightful Messiah.

He will reign over the house of Jacob forever. "House of Jacob" was frequently used to describe Israel. Like David, Jesus is the King of Israel. His kingdom has already begun, but unlike other kingdoms, it will last forever.

His kingdom will never end. The eternal nature of the David kingship was taught in 2 Samuel 7:13–16. "Your house and kingdom will endure before Me forever, and your throne will be established forever" (verse 16). No earthly king was ever able to fulfill this promise. This prophecy could only be fulfilled by one who is from everlasting to everlasting.

It is tragic to think that the majority of the Jewish people have never seriously considered the claims of the Son of the Most High. Have you ever told one of your Jewish friends about their rightful King?

GOD WILL
ESTABLISH JUSTICE

> **Luke 18:8** I tell you that He
> will swiftly grant them justice.

Have you ever found yourself thinking
that the world isn't fair? When you see the
wicked getting ahead, do you ever wonder
if there will ever be justice on earth? Do
you sometimes think that your prayers are
bouncing off your ceiling unanswered?
This promise will encourage you to remain
faithful to God and persistent in prayer.

Jesus began this section by telling a
parable designed to encourage his disciples
to pray and not lose heart. The two charac-
ters in the parable are a judge "who didn't
fear God or respect man" (verse 2) and a
needy widow. We are told on two occasions
that the judge did not fear God; therefore,
we do not expect him to show mercy and
grant protection to her or to anyone else.
Yet the defenseless widow kept coming to
the judge seeking legal protection from her
opponent. The unjust judge responded to
the widow's request simply because she

persistently bothered him. He feared she would wear him out.

The question and the point are both obvious. If an unjust judge grants justice to the widow, how much more readily will God, who is perfectly just, "grant justice to His elect who cry to Him day and night?" (verse 7). Will God be patient for very much longer while his people suffer and cry out to him in prayer? The obvious answer is that he will "swiftly" bring about justice for them.

He then posed a question designed to spur the disciples on to faithfulness and perseverance in prayer, "Nevertheless, when the Son of Man comes, will He find that faith on earth?" (verse 8). The point of the parable is not whether or not God will respond to prayer, but whether his disciples will be faithful and persist in prayer while the Son of Man tarries.

Thus, this parable is an encouragement for us to persevere in prayer. We can rely on God to answer the prayer of the faithful and to bring justice. Do you pray with persistence? Be encouraged that he will bring about justice.

GOD WILL
RISE AGAIN

{
Luke 18:33 After they flog
Him, they will kill Him, and He
will rise on the third day.
}

The rich young ruler walked away
having rejected Christ. His love of wealth
kept him from making the one decision that
could have given him true wealth. Jesus
then told the disciples that it is difficult for
the wealthy to enter the kingdom of God.

The disciples could hardly believe what
they were hearing. They may have been
like many of their day who saw wealth as a
sign of God's blessing. The wealthy could
give more alms for the poor. If this man
can't be saved, who can? The answer is
simple. God can do the impossible. He can
break our addiction to wealth.

This event caused the disciples to
wonder about the sacrifice they had made
to follow Jesus. But Jesus promised that
no sacrifice can compare with the reward
of knowing him. It is in this context that
Jesus took the disciples aside to give them
a sketch of what lay ahead.

He indicated that what was to happen would fulfill all the things written by the prophets, referring to the entirety of the Old Testament. This reference to prophecy assured the disciples that God would be the one bringing it about.

Jesus was to be handed over, mocked, mistreated, spit upon, and flogged. I had never thought much about the flogging of Jesus until I attended *The Passion of the Christ* by Mel Gibson. I found myself often turning my eyes away from the screen. It was difficult to comprehend the hatred that was poured out upon Jesus. What made it so difficult to watch was the knowledge that he took my place. He did this for me!

The scourging was not the end of man's cruelty—"they will kill Him." When you consider the care and compassion demonstrated by Jesus in his earthly ministry, it is difficult to comprehend that men would put him to death. Yet his death was part of God's plan for our redemption.

The story does not end here. "He will rise on the third day." The scourging and death of Jesus was neither mistake nor tragedy. It was divine necessity.

GOD WILL
HELP US UNDERSTAND

{ **John 4:25** When He comes, He will explain everything to us. }

Have you ever longed for a friend to whom you could reveal you deepest secrets without fear of betrayal or recrimination? What if this friend had the power to forgive and transform?

The story of the Samaritan woman at the well is a favorite of many. Jesus approached a woman who had three strikes against her in the climate of her day. She was a woman, a despised half-breed (a Samaritan), and had a reputation for immoral behavior. Jesus accepted water from her, then offered *her* a gift of water that would cure her deepest thirst in life.

When Jesus revealed his knowledge that the woman had previously had five husbands, she concluded that he was a prophet (verse 19). Perhaps to move the attention away from her present condition, she decided to debate with him the proper place of worship. The Samaritans based their worship at Gerizim on Deuteronomy 11:29. Jesus ignored the "place" debate to speak about the quality of true worship.

This fallen woman revealed the longing of her heart when she declared the words of verse 25. The Samaritans expected a Messiah, but not one from the Davidic line. They were expecting a Moses-like figure who could explain everything to them (Deut. 18:15–18). Was she hoping the Messiah would put an end to all disputes, supply all our defects, and tell us the mind of God? Was she genuinely looking for the Messianic age, or was she making a last ditch effort to change the subject?

It may be that there was an anxious combination of both. It is possible that this woman, wounded by the men she had encountered, was unwilling to reveal herself fully until she was sure it was safe to do so. Jesus' response is direct and profound—"I am He, the One speaking to you" (verse 26). Jesus is the Messiah!

Today, you can reveal your inmost fears and aspirations to the one who alone declares all things. He is faithful and true, ready to listen and to help us understand.

GOD WILL
GIVE YOU A HELPER

{ **John 14:16** I will ask the
Father, and He will give you
another Counselor to be
with you forever. }

I grew up in Thomasville, North
Carolina, home of Mills Home orphanage.
I had many friends who lived there. One of
them expressed to me the agony of being
an orphan. He explained that when he
graduated from high school, he would be
on his own. He had no family and no
means of support. He had no "helper."

Jesus had just told his disciples that he
would be leaving them, and that they could
not follow him now (John 13:36). He had
called them to a radical lifestyle, requiring
them to love each other as he had loved
them (13:34–35). He must have shaken
their world when he promised that they
would do greater works than he had done
simply because he was going to the Father
(14:12). The commandment calling them to
radical love and the possibility of "greater
works" would necessitate resources of
divine proportions.

So Jesus promised them a "Counselor" or "Helper." Jesus had been their helper during his earthly ministry. But he knew his disciples needed "another"—a helper who would be with them forever.

The Greek word used here is often transliterated as *paraclete*. This can be translated as "comforter," "advocate," or "helper." The *paraclete* is one who pleads your case and is called alongside to give aid. Jesus had certainly fulfilled this role during his earthly ministry. But with the departure of Jesus, the Father was prepared to send a helper who would be with them at all times and all places.

Jesus identified the Comforter as the Spirit of truth who resided within them. In the Old Testament period, the Spirit came upon people to produce mighty acts, but he did not indwell them. The disciples, however, would not be orphaned after Jesus' departure. He would come to them in the outpouring of the Spirit at Pentecost.

If you are a Christian, this promise of an indwelling Helper applies to you. Are you aware of his presence? Do you invite him to infill and guide you?

GOD WILL
TESTIFY ABOUT HIMSELF

> **John 15:26** When the
> Counselor comes . . . He
> will testify about Me.

Do you ever find yourself strangely silent when it comes to telling others about your personal relationship to Christ? If so, you are not alone. Statistics tell us that only a very small percentage of born again believers have ever told anyone about their relationship with Christ. Would it help you to know that you have a Helper who will join you as you share?

In our last section, we looked at Jesus' promise that he would send a "Counselor" or "Helper" who would enable the disciples to accomplish greater works than Jesus had done. In the next several sections, we will look at the ministry of our Helper.

It is not insignificant that this promise is in the context of the warning that the world will often be hostile to the Christian and his message. One source of this hostility is related to the issue of sin. "If I had not come and spoken to them," Jesus said, "they would not have sin. Now they have no excuse for their sin" (verse 22). Jesus' coming and his message confronted man with his sinfulness and his need for a Savior. This was not a popular message in Jesus' day, and it remains unpopular today. We want to blame our circumstances for our failing rather than confront our own sinfulness.

Yet the disciples were encouraged by the promise of a Helper who would testify about Jesus. The work of the Son was to glorify the Father, and the work of the Spirit was to testify to the Son. In verse 27, Jesus further clarified the work of the Holy Spirit with this declaration: "You also will testify." Yes, the Spirit bears witness to Christ through human instrumentation. As we tell our story, the Holy Spirit testifies to the Son through us.

When we share the gospel with others, the Holy Spirit persuades them of their sin and their need, as well as the truth of our witness. The result is that people are saved. It is your responsibility to tell your kingdom story; it is the work of the Spirit to bring conviction.

GOD WILL
EXPOSE HUMAN SIN

> **John 16:8** When He comes, He will convict the world about sin, righteousness, and judgment.

We continue our look at the ministry of the Holy Spirit. This "God Will" promise helps us understand how the Holy Spirit will empower our witnessing by bringing conviction to the world. Notice that there is a triad of conviction:

He will convict the world concerning "sin" because the world does not believe in him. This issue of sin is not so much the choice of erroneous acts but the fundamental act of rejecting Christ and choosing another god. When one refuses to believe in Christ, he has called the Spirit a liar and rejected God's own Son. This is the essence of sin, and self is at the heart of it. This is the rebellion we saw in the Garden when Adam and Eve desired to be like God.

The Holy Spirit will convict the world of the "righteousness" of Jesus. When the Jews and the crowd called for Jesus' crucifixion, they were declaring that Jesus was a wicked person. According to Deuteronomic Law, only a wicked person could be hanged on a tree (Deut. 21:23). You may wonder what the reference of Jesus going to the Father has to do with the conviction of righteousness. It speaks of the resurrection and ascension of Jesus. The fact that they no longer see him on earth indicates that he is in the presence of a righteous God. Since God cannot allow unrighteousness into heaven, the ascension is solemn declaration of Jesus' righteousness.

The Holy Spirit will convict the world concerning "judgment" because the ruler of this world has been judged. The death and subsequent resurrection of Jesus was the ultimate defeat of the devil, who held the power of death. Now that death has been defeated, the ruler of this world has been judged and declared guilty.

People in rebellion should take note of Satan's defeat and should turn to the Lord. The prince of this world stands condemned, and so will all those who stand with him and reject Christ. When you share your kingdom story, you can trust the Holy Spirit to bring conviction.

GOD WILL
GUIDE YOU INTO TRUTH

> **John 16:13** When the Spirit of truth comes, He will guide you into all the truth.

Have you ever been out hiking and lost your way? Even landmarks that once looked familiar now seem strange and foreboding. During a time like this, we desire and need a guide, someone who has been there and can guide us without error.

The disciples had been grieved and confused by the announcement of Jesus' departure. They were still preoccupied with their own positions in an earthly kingdom. Their grief and introverted focus was a barrier to receiving more spiritual truth at this point. Jesus, recognizing the confusion of the disciples, declared: "I still have many things to tell you, but you can't bear them now" (verse 12).

The good news is that everything lacking in their spiritual education would be resolved when the Spirit of truth came. His task was to guide them into all truth, giving them insight into the meaning of the events soon to come. They would be given clear insight into the rejection of the Messiah and the accompanying events of the cross and resurrection. That's because the Spirit does not speak on his own initiative; he speaks only those things the Father reveals to Him. He is not some nebulous force or power; he is the third person of the triune God.

The Spirit glorifies the Son in the same manner that the Son glorified the Father. We see here the unity and interrelatedness of the triune God. This final promise is beautiful and encouraging: "Everything the Father has is Mine. This is why I told you that He takes from what is Mine and will declare it to you" (verse 15). Can you believe that the Father loves us this much? All the resources of the Father have been given to the Son, and the Spirit will disclose the resources of heaven to us.

The Spirit enabled the early disciples to understand all the truths about the Savior. The good news is that this same Spirit is available to believers today. When you read the Scripture, the Holy Spirit will guide you into all truth.

GOD WILL
ANSWER YOUR PRAYERS

> **John 16:23** I assure you:
> Anything you ask the Father
> in My name, He will give you.

This verse has caused some people to treat the phrase "in Jesus' name" as a magical formula assuring us that every prayer request will be granted. This misunderstanding has led to confusion and disappointment as desired requests were seemingly denied even when prayed with the appropriate formula.

Jesus was encouraging his disciples with the assurance that his earthly departure would be to their advantage, ushering in the new age in which the Holy Spirit would indwell them. The coming of this new age would transform the disciples' means and mode of communication. Their queries and requests would no longer be directed to the earthly Jesus. They would now direct all requests directly to the Father through Jesus' name.

The phrase "in Jesus' name" was never intended to be a magic wand assuring that we get our every request like spoiled children in a candy store. Further, it is not a last ditch effort for poorly thought out requests, a sort of blank check assurance that we can pray careless prayers and still have our wishes fulfilled. What, then, does is mean to pray in Jesus' name?

First, to pray in Jesus' name means that the person praying has an intimate and personal relationship with Jesus. I live in a community where you can charge food based on your name. When my children visit, they also have the privilege of charging their food to my name and account. I don't afford that right to just anyone, only my children. Praying in Jesus' name indicates personal relationship with Christ (see Acts 4:12).

Second, it means that the prayer will reflect Jesus' character. You could paraphrase a familiar question in a slightly different way—"What would Jesus pray?"

Third, it will be focused on manifesting the character of God, advancing the kingdom of God and accomplishing the will of God (see Matt. 6:9–13).

When you pray "in his name," you can be assured your prayers will be answered.

GOD WILL
DISTRIBUTE GIFTS TO US

> **1 Corinthians 12:11** One and
> the same Spirit is active in all
> these, distributing to each
> one as He wills.

One of the most painful memories of
my early childhood was school recess when
we chose up sides to play a sporting event.
I was what my dad called a "late bloomer."
I was relatively small until I finally hit my
growth spurt. So I was occasionally not
chosen in the early rounds of the grade
school "draft." Such an event can cause
you to feel rejected and of little value. I
have found that many Christians feel as if
they are of little value to their church or to
the kingdom of God. If you sometimes feel
that way, this kingdom promise is for you.

Spiritual gifts had caused much confusion in Corinth, creating both pain and
pride. Some felt their "superior" gifts
proved them to be spiritually elite, while
others believed themselves to be without
gifts altogether. Paul corrected both errors.
To those who thought gifts proved them to
be spiritual, Paul declared that gifts are

essentially a manifestation of God's grace and therefore tell us nothing about the recipient but everything about the giver. To those who thought themselves devoid of all gifts, he assured them that all believers have received the Spirit and therefore all alike share in his gifts. "A manifestation of the Spirit is given to each person to produce what is beneficial" (verse 7).

Let's underline three truths. *First, you have the Spirit, and thus you are gifted.* Paul made it clear that one cannot belong to Christ and not have the Spirit. "If anyone does not have the Spirit of Christ, he does not belong to Him" (Rom. 8:9).

Second, you are gifted for service to the King through his body. That is what Paul meant when he spoke of the Spirit being given for the common good.

Third, you have precisely the gift or gifts the King desires you to have. "God has placed the parts, each one of them, in the body just as He wanted" (verse 18).

Once we understand these fundamental truths about gifts, we understand that our singular purpose in life is to serve and please the King.

GOD WILL
PROTECT US FROM EVIL

{ **2 Thessalonians 3:3** The Lord is faithful; He will strengthen and guard you from the evil one. }

My granddaughters love to play games in which they are princesses living in a time when there were dragons and monsters. What I like best about their games is that when they're over at our house, their play often leads them to come to their "papa" for protection. They know I'll keep them safe from all mythical creatures.

Paul was able to tell the troubled Thessalonian believers that the Lord would protect them from the evil one. Like their founding pastor, these men and women had experienced various trials, including being persecuted for their faith. In the two verses prior to this kingdom promise, Paul had requested prayer from the Thessalonians for himself and his coworkers. Paul asked that they pray for God's Word to continue to spread rapidly and be received by others, and that the missionaries would be rescued from evil men.

In our focal verse, Paul turned from consideration of his own needs to those of the Thessalonians. His assurance that the early Christians would experience strength and protection is based on a fundamental truth—"The Lord is faithful." In other words, God can be trusted even in the face of persecution and difficulty. His faithfulness ensures that he is at work in the midst of our suffering, that he will ultimately bring judgment on all evil, and that our days are secure in him.

Persecution by faithless persons was a stark reality for members of the early Christian church. Thus, the declaration of God's faithfulness and the assurance of strength and protection must have greatly encouraged these new believers. You may have noticed, both in this text and in real life, God's protection does not mean the absence of conflict and suffering. It does, however, promise strength and preservation in the midst of the suffering. The "evil one" may be a general reference to evil or to Satan himself. In either case, it is comforting and encouraging to know that we have God's protection.

GOD WILL
RETURN TO EARTH

> **1 Timothy 6:14–15** Keep the
> commandment . . . until the
> appearing of our Lord . . .
> which God will bring about.

The Lord's return has long been a topic
of fascination, speculation, and sometimes
division in the Christian community. But
how tragic that such a profound truth
would ever cause disunity among us. The
assurance of his victorious return ought
always be seen as a magnificent assurance
with profound impact on our daily living.

The promise of the Lord's sure and
victorious return is found in a section
where Paul was issuing a solemn charge
to Timothy. His specific charge was that
Timothy would "keep the commandment
without spot or blame." It is likely this
"commandment" refers to the specific
concerns mentioned in the present context,
particularly verses 11 and 12. Timothy had
been exhorted to flee certain behaviors and
pursue righteousness, godliness, faith, love,
perseverance, and gentleness, enabling him
to fight the good fight of faith.

Like Timothy, we are called to "fight the good fight" and "keep the commandment without spot or blame" until the appearing of our Lord Jesus Christ. His return is assured, ready to be accomplished by God himself "in His own time." In Galatians 4:4, Paul told us that God sent his Son at the "fullness of time" or the "completion of the time." Now we are told that God will send him again in God's perfect time. This may have been a subtle rebuke to those who thought they could calculate the time of the Lord's return.

With such a glorious thought in mind, Paul broke forth in a magnificent doxology—"He is the blessed and only Sovereign, the King of kings, and the Lord of lords, the only One who has immortality, dwelling in unapproachable light" (verses 15–16).

This passage assures us that Christ's certain return will occur at precisely the right time and will be accomplished by divine activity. Rather than speculating about the specifics of his return, we should be encouraged to live faithfully and serve him with diligence.

GOD WILL
DRAW NEAR TO YOU

> **James 4:8** Draw near to God, and He will draw near to you.

When I was a child, I hungered for intimacy with my parents. Their embrace brought a sense of comfort and security. The child of God longs for intimacy with God, and thus we are encouraged by this invitation that doubles as a command.

James had just told his readers; "God resists the proud, but gives grace to the humble" (verse 6). He followed this with two imperatives—"Submit to God. But resist the Devil, and he will flee from you" (verse 7). There is an obvious and natural progression in the text that we must follow if we long for intimacy with God.

The first step to intimacy is the absolute submission of our will to God's. When the kingdom of God comes in fullness, everything in heaven and on earth will be in absolute submission to God (1 Cor. 15:27). Thus, it is appropriate that kingdom citizens subordinate their lives to the King.

Step two is to resist the devil. Our attitude toward God is one of absolute surrender; therefore, our attitude toward his arch-enemy is just the opposite. Evil is not approached with indifference or with timidity; it is resisted with assured victory.

It is at this point that we find the verse assuring us of God's presence. This promise does not suggest that the initiative of intimacy lies with us. God has always been the initiator of intimacy with man. It is rather the assurance that when we come to him, we will always find him waiting to forgive and receive us. It also reminds us that often when we sense that God is far away, the distance is the result of our sinful departure.

Two more imperatives follow this promise—"cleanse your hands" and "purify your hearts." The two acts we looked at previously were *necessary* for drawing near; the two now in consideration are the *result* of drawing near. Both the cleansing of the hands and the purifying of the heart are preparation for service. When we truly draw near to God, our singular desire is to serve him.

GOD WILL
EXALT YOU

{ **James 4:10** Humble yourselves
before the Lord, and He
will exalt you. }

Micah, the Old Testament prophet,
effectively summarized a purposeful life—
"to act justly, to love faithfulness, and to
walk humbly with your God" (Micah 6:8).
James echoed this theme that humility
before the rightful King is the path to
meaningful life and appropriate reward.

What, then, does it mean to humble
ourselves? It is not a pious self-deprecation
which actually serves to draw attention to
oneself. No, we are humbled the moment
we properly understand the majesty of the
King and our unworthiness to come into
his presence. The humble know that even
at our best, we are still sinners by nature
and practice. When the Holy Spirit reveals
the glory of the King and the depth of our
sin, humble submission naturally follows.

Humility acknowledges that grace
alone enables us to stand in the presence of
holy God. The very fact that a sinful man

could be invited into the presence of the King is a sobering reality that brings us to our knees in gratitude. But true humility will not stop here. It naturally leads to our desire to submit our wills to his perfect will and to serve him with all we are and all we have. It recognizes the King's rightful claim to all of our lives. It will lead us to practice humility in our treatment of others, seeking the way of unrecognized service rather than exalted prominence.

Humility is maintained as we understand that all of life—every day and every moment—is lived in the presence of the King. This understanding means the King values us and holds us accountable for representing him on planet earth.

And the end result of such kingdom-focused living is this: "He will exalt you." The promise of reward is not an enticement to serve; it is an affirmation of the rightness of kingdom living. Service to the King may go unnoticed for now, bringing persecution and temporal loss (see Mark 10:30), but in the eternal kingdom, it will be rewarded by the King himself. Never trade temporal recognition for eternal reward.

GOD WILL
REIGN FOREVER AND EVER

> **Revelation 11:15** The kingdom
> of the world has become the
> kingdom of our Lord . . . and
> He will reign forever and ever!

I was in college during the conflict in
Vietnam. Many of my classmates despaired
about the future. The conflict today with
terrorists on every front has created a new
sense of despair and hopelessness. Can
anyone make any sense out of world events
and give meaning to life?

The kingdom promise above comes
from the last book of the Bible. The sev-
enth trumpet has sounded, and the loud
voices of the heavenly hosts declare the
replacement of the kingdom of the world
by the kingdom of our Lord and of his
Christ. We sometimes forget that Scripture
informs us that the present world order is
already on its way to dissolution. Now the
heavenly hosts declare that the final victory
has been accomplished and God's kingdom
is becoming visible for all to see.

You may have noticed that "kingdom
of the world" is singular, suggesting that

behind all earthly powers is a singular source of authority—the adversary himself. Our text does not focus on the power of the adversary, however, but on the assured victory of the King. God has always been sovereign and his victory certain. Now his plan has been brought to final consummation for all to see. The rebellion of evil has finally been eradicated and God's kingdom has been established on earth.

John spoke of Christ's victory as a present reality—which it is! His victorious return will only serve to make visible what kingdom-focused people already know to be true. The present world is temporary, but his coming kingdom is "forever and ever."

The writer of Hebrews stated this same truth when he spoke of the "shaking" that would bring all created things and earthly kingdoms to an end. His conclusion— "Since we are receiving a kingdom that cannot be shaken, let us hold on to grace. By it, we may serve God acceptably, with reverence and awe" (Heb. 12:28). The assured victory of our King not only gives us assured hope; it also calls us to service.

GOD WILL
DWELL AMONG US

> **Revelation 21:3** Look! God's dwelling is with men, and He will live with them.

Sometimes when flying, I look out on the clouds and wonder what heaven will be like. Revelation 21 gives us a rare glimpse concerning the glory and grandeur of that kingdom when everything is transformed. John is limited in his ability to describe the kingdom by his earthly vocabulary. Thus, he simply states that there will be "a new heaven and a new earth" (verse 1). He is not implying a better edition of what we already know. Rather, there will no longer be any separation between heaven and earth, or between man and his King.

If you read chapter 21 in its totality, you will see that the primary focus is on the presence of God. Nothing can exceed the affirmation that God is present. The use of the word "dwelling" or "tabernacle" is interesting, too. It may be used to contrast the temporary nature of worship in the moveable tent from Old Testament days.

More likely, it is intended to recall the Hebrew word that we transliterate as *shekinah*, a term that denotes both God's glory and his presence.

It is beyond our earthly comprehension to think that we, as children of the King, will one day dwell with him in all of his glory. You may recall that this is precisely what Jesus asked for his disciples in his final High Priestly prayer. "Father, I desire those You have given Me to be with Me where I am. Then they will see My glory, which You have given Me" (John 17:24). The prayer and the promise have now become reality.

There is nothing impersonal about dwelling in his presence. "He will wipe away every tear from their eyes. Death will exist no longer; grief, crying, and pain will exist no longer, because the previous things have passed away" (verse 4). Imagine such intimate personal care by the King of kings and Lord of lords!

You simply cannot afford to miss this kingdom. It is accessed only through Jesus Christ. If you are not certain, turn the page and follow the directions.

APPENDIX

The promises of this book are based on one's relationship to Christ. If you have not yet entered a personal relationship with Jesus Christ, I encourage you to make this wonderful discovery today. I like to use the very simple acrostic—LIFE—to explain this, knowing that God wants you not only to inherit *eternal* life but also to experience *earthly* life to its fullest.

L = LOVE

It all begins with God's love. God created you in his image. This means you were created to live in relationship with him. *"For God loved the world in this way: He gave His One and Only Son, so that everyone who believes in Him will not perish but have eternal life"* (John 3:16).

But if God loves you and desires a relationship with you, why do you feel so isolated from him?

I = ISOLATION

This isolation is created by our sin—our rebellion against God—which separates us from him and from others. *"For all have sinned and fall short of the glory of God"* (Rom. 3:23). *"For the wages of sin is death, but the gift of God is eternal life in Christ Jesus our Lord"* (Rom. 6:23).

You might wonder how you can overcome this isolation and have an intimate relationship with God.

F = FORGIVENESS

The only solution to man's isolation and separation from a holy God is forgiveness. *"For Christ also suffered for sins once for all, the righteous for the unrighteous, that He might bring you to God, after being put to death in the fleshly realm but made alive in the spiritual realm"* (1 Pet. 3:18).

The only way our relationship can be restored with God is through the forgiveness of our sins. Jesus Christ died on the cross for this very purpose.

E = ETERNAL LIFE

You can have full and abundant life in this present life . . . and eternal life when you die. *"But to all who did receive Him, He gave them the right to be children of God, to those who believe in His name"* (John 1:12). *"A thief comes only to steal and to kill and to destroy. I have come that they may have life and have it in abundance"* (John 10:10).

Is there any reason you wouldn't like to have a personal relationship with God?

THE PLAN OF SALVATION

It's as simple as ABC. All you have to do is:

A = Admit you are a sinner. Turn from your sin and turn to God. *"Repent and turn back, that your sins may be wiped out so that seasons of refreshing may come from the presence of the Lord"* (Acts 3:19).

B = Believe that Jesus died for your sins and rose from the dead enabling you to have life. *"I have written these things to you who believe in the name of the Son of God, so that you may know that you have eternal life"* (1 John 5:13).

C = Confess verbally and publicly your belief in Jesus Christ. *"If you confess with your mouth, 'Jesus is Lord,' and believe in your heart that God raised Him from the dead, you will be saved. With the heart one believes, resulting in righteousness, and with the mouth one confesses, resulting in salvation"* (Rom. 10:9–10).

You can invite Jesus Christ to come into your life right now. Pray something like this:

"God, I admit that I am a sinner. I believe that you sent Jesus, who died on the cross and rose from the dead, paying the penalty for my sins. I am asking that you forgive me of my sin, and I receive your gift of eternal life. It is in Jesus' name that I ask for this gift. Amen."

Signed _____

Date _____

If you have a friend or family member who is a Christian, tell them about your decision. Then find a church that teaches the Bible, and let them help you go deeper with Christ.

KINGDOM PROMISES

If you've enjoyed this book of Kingdom
Promises, you may want to consider
reading one of the others in the series:

 God Is
978-0-8054-4766-8

 We Are
978-0-8054-2783-7

 We Can
978-0-8054-2780-6

 But God
978-0-8054-2782-0

Available in stores nationwide and through
major online retailers. For a complete look
at Ken Hemphill titles, make sure to visit
www.bhpublishinggroup.com/hemphill.